If your friends come over to play, what do you say?

Hello!

If someone gives you something nice,
what do you say?

Thank you!

If things go wrong while you're having fun, what do you say?

I'm sorry!

If you would like something, what do you say?

Please!

EAU CLAIRE DISTRICT LIBRARY

If that sneeze takes you by surprise,
what do you say?

If you make a naughty noise,
what do you say?

Pardon me!

If it's just a great big treat,
what do you say?

If someone is cheating,
what do you say?

Play fair!

If you leave a really big mess,
what do you say?

Clean up time!

When your party comes to an end,
what do you say?

Remember "please" and "thank you," too,

and lots of hugs will come to you!

EAU CLAIRE DISTRICT LIBRARY

to Jayne and the Bump!

First edition for the United States, its dependencies, the Philippines, and
Canada published by Barron's Educational Series, Inc. 2002

First published in Great Britain in 2002 by Red Fox
an imprint of Random House Children's Books

Copyright © Richard Morgan 2002

The right of Richard Morgan to be identified as the author and illustrator of this work
has been asserted by him in accordance with the Copyright, Designs and Patents Act, 1988.

All rights reserved. No part of this book may be reproduced in any form, by photostat,
microfilm, xerography, or any other means, or incorporated into any information
retrieval system, electronic or mechanical, without the written permission
of the copyright owner.

All inquiries should be addressed to:
Barron's Educational Series, Inc.
250 Wireless Boulevard
Hauppauge, New York 11788
http://www.barronseduc.com

International Standard Book No. 0-7641-2287-8

Library of Congress Catalog Card No. 2002101634

Printed in Singapore
9 8 7 6 5 4 3 2 1